NINJA AIR FRYER COOKBOOK FOR BEGINNERS:

Easy and Healthy Ninja Air Fryer Recipes.

By
Helena Clark

© Copyright by Helena Clark 2024 - All rights reserved.

The content contained within this book may not be reproduced, duplicated or transmitted without direct written permission from the author or the publisher.

Under no circumstances will any blame or legal responsibility be held against the publisher, or author, for any damages, reparation, or monetary loss due to the information contained within this book. Either directly or indirectly. You are responsible for your own choices, actions, and results.

Legal Notice:
This book is copyright protected. This book is only for personal use. You cannot amend, distribute, sell, use, quote or paraphrase any part, or the content within this book, without the consent of the author or publisher.

Disclaimer Notice:
Please note the information contained within this document is for educational and entertainment purposes only. All effort has been executed to present accurate, up to date, and reliable, complete information. No warranties of any kind are declared or implied. Readers acknowledge that the author is not engaging in the rendering of legal, financial, medical or professional advice. The content within this book has been derived from various sources. Please consult a licensed professional before attempting any techniques outlined in this book.

By reading this document, the reader agrees that under no circumstances is the author responsible for any losses, direct or indirect, which are incurred as a result of the use of the information contained within this document, including, but not limited to, — errors, omissions, or inaccuracies.

TABLE OF CONTENTS

INTRODUCTION 7
Benefits and Advantages of an Air Fryer 9
How to air fry your food in an air fryer? 10
Functions of Air Fryer 11

BREAKFAST RECIPES 13
Fruit Flapjack 14
Broccoli Breakfast Bake 14
Healthy Breakfast Bars 15
Cheesy Hash Brown Cups 15
Apple Breakfast Bake 16
Greek Spinach Egg Cups 16
Baked Egg Quiche 17
Breakfast Muffins 17
Juicy Breakfast Meat Patties 18
Stuffed Bell Peppers 18

LUNCH RECIPES 19
Greek Baby Potatoes 20
Creamy Turnip Gratin 20
Aubergine Gratin 21
Greek Tilapia 21
Quick Baked Cod 22
Lemon Pepper Basa 22
Turkey Patties 23
Herb Chicken Breasts 23
Marinated Chicken Breasts 24
Turkey Spinach Patties 24

APPETIZERS & SIDE DISHES 25
Perfect Garlic Bread 26
Healthy & Tasty Butternut Squash 26
Garlic Parmesan Cauliflower 27
Crispy Broccoli Tots 27
Banana Chips 28
Brussels Sprout Chips 28
Onion Dip 29
Baked Chicken Meatballs 29
Crispy Potato Fries 30
Roasted Cashews 30

FISH & SEAFOOD RECIPES 31
Perfect Salmon Patties 32
Simple & Quick Salmon 32
Crab Patties 33
Quick Scallop Gratin 33
Baked Dijon Salmon 34
Healthy Baked Cod 34
Shrimp Casserole 35
Rosemary Garlic Shrimp.. 35
Quick & Spicy Shrimp 36
Greek Salmon 36

POULTRY RECIPES 37
Juicy Chicken Breasts 38
Southwest Chicken Breasts.. 38
Meatballs 39
Juicy Turkey Patties 39
Chicken Jerky.. 40
Baked Meatballs 40
Balsamic Chicken 41
Creamy Chicken Breasts 41
Cheesy Chicken Broccoli 42
Baked Chicken Thighs 42
Spiced Chicken Wings.. 43
Cheesy Chicken Patties 43
Tasty Chicken Wings.. 44
Turkey Meatballs 44
Cajun Herb Chicken Thighs 45
Juicy Turkey Patties 45
Spiced Chicken Thighs 46
Greek Chicken Meatballs 46
Jalapeno Chicken Meatballs 47
Greek Chicken Breast.. 47

MEAT RECIPES... 48
Meatballs... 49
Juicy & Tender Pork Chops 49
Garlic Butter Pork Chops 50
Tasty Lamb Patties 50
Meatballs 51
Garlic Mint Lamb Chops... 51
Mustard Lamb Chops 52
Balsamic Lamb Chops.. 52

Garlic Sage Pork Chops 53
Steak Bites with Veggie 53
Lemon Garlic Pork Chops 54
Honey Mustard Pork Chops 54
Sweet & Spicy Pork Chops 55
Mexican Meat Patties 55
Beef Jerky 56
Meatballs 56
Herb Pork Chops 57
Marinated Pork ribs 57
Meatballs 58
Pork Jerky 58

VEGETABLE RECIPES 59
Courgette Casserole 60
Baked Brussels Sprouts 60
Healthy Baked Vegetables 61
Cheesy Courgette Bake 61
Carrot Courgette Patties 62
Crispy Cauliflower Florets 62
Garlic Mushrooms 63
Spinach Quinoa Patties 63
Crispy Sweet Potato Wedges 64
Tomato Slices 64

DESSERTS 65
Tender & Sweet Cinnamon Apples 66
Delicious Berry Brownie 66
Date Brownies 67
Vanilla Berry Cobbler 67
Orange Muffins 68
Almond Butter Banana Brownie 68
Dehydrated Mango Slices 69
Banana Muffins 69
Dehydrated Apple Slices 70
Kiwi Slices 70

CONCLUSION 71

INTRODUCTION

A Ninja air fryer is a handy cooking device that is capable of cooking a variety of foods in one appliance. You can use the Ninja air fryer for maximum crisp, air fry, air roast, bake, air broil, reheat, and dehydrate your favourite food. One of the great things about using a Ninja air fryer is that it needs very little fats and oils to cook your food. It uses 80 to 90 percent less fats and oils than the traditional deep frying method. This ensures that fewer calories, less fat, and fewer harmful compounds are present in your food. If you enjoy fried food, using the Ninja air fryer is a healthy and diet-friendly way to fry your food without changing its texture and taste like deep-fried food does. It allows you to make healthier versions of your beloved fried dishes. Air-fried food is a healthier option than traditionally fried food, which is unhealthy.

The air fryer cooks tasty and healthy food by using fast heat circulation. A heating element makes heat, and a fan spreads it in the cooking chamber for even cooking.

Whether you're making a big family meal or a quick snack for yourself, let the Ninja Air Fryer Cookbook be your guide. Say goodbye to boring cooking days and welcome a world of crispy, tender, and yummy meals that you and your loved ones will love. Have fun with your air-frying adventures!

This cookbook has 100 yummy and healthy air fryer recipes covering breakfast to desserts. The recipes are unique and good for you. Each recipe mentions prep and cook time, with step-by-step instructions. Nutritional info at the end helps you keep track of your daily calorie intake. Many cookbooks talk about this, so thanks for choosing mine. I hope you enjoy all the recipes in this cookbook.

Benefits and Advantages of an Air Fryer

One of the healthiest ways to prepare your favourite foods is to air fry them. Numerous benefits and advantages come with using an air fryer. Some of the few significant benefits and advantages of air fryers include:

- *Healthier cooking method:* One of the best things about air fryers is that they make cooking healthier. It uses less oil than traditional frying; thus, the amount of fat in your food is reduced. Less oil and fat helps to lower your daily caloric intake and keep you fit and healthy. This is beneficial if you're attempting to reduce your intake of calories and bad fats.

- *Use less fats and oil:* To get crispy food, air fryers only use a small amount of oil, sometimes none at all. This implies that you may indulge in the crunch without consuming excessive amounts of bad fat. Both your health and your taste senses will benefit from it!

- *Quick and even cooking:* The Air fryer cooks your favourite food by circulating very hot air around the frying chamber with the help of a convection fan. Every time, an even dispersion of hot air into the cooking chamber results in faster and more evenly cooked food. If you have a busy daily schedule and do not have enough time to prepare your meals, then the air fryer allows you to cook your food more quickly and evenly.

- *Keeps nutrients intact*: When you deep fry food, you often lose many of its healthy nutrients, and it can even create harmful chemicals. However, an air fryer uses a fast, hot air circulation method and needs very little fat and oil. Your food gets cooked by hot air swirling around it, keeping the essential nutrients intact.

- *Versatile cooking appliances:* An air fryer is like a superhero in your kitchen – it can do lots of things. It can air fry, bake, broil, roast, and dehydrate your food. The specific air fryer model you pick will decide what it's best at. Having a multipurpose gadget like this air fryer means you don't have to go out and buy different tools for each cooking task.

- *Safe to use:* Most of the air fryers come with an overheating prevention feature for safety reasons. The majority of air fryers automatically turn off when the countdown hits zero. Air fryers include a 360-degree closing mechanism that eliminates the possibility of hot oil splashing, spilling, or accidental touch.

- *Easy to operate:* The control panel system on the air fryer is very easy to operate. Everything you need to prepare is listed on the control panel. All you have to do is load the food basket with your favourite foods, secure it inside the air fryer, and select the appropriate cooking setting as per your recipe needs.

How to air fry your food in an air fryer?

If you're new to air frying, then following the step-by-step guide will assist you in quickly creating healthy and tasty air-fried recipes.

1. ***Prepare your food:*** Food preparation is one of the important things that starts before the cooking process. It involves tasks like washing, slicing, peeling, mixing, grinding, and cutting your ingredients and vegetables. Doing these things ahead of time not only saves you lots of time but also allows you to control your portion size.

2. ***Grease food basket:*** Always grease your food basket using the best quality cooking spray. Make sure all the sides are covered properly and the bottom thoroughly before you put your food into the food basket. This simple step stops your food from sticking and makes cleaning up a breeze.

3. ***Preheat the Air Fryer:*** This is one of the most important steps to achieving uniform and rapid cooking. It also helps to crisp up your food and save cooking time. In general, your air fryer only needs three minutes to preheat your air fryer.

4. ***Place food into the basket:*** Place your food pieces into the food basket in such a way that leaves room between them. Don't overcrowd food in a basket; it may give you uneven cooking results.

5. ***Set time and temperature:*** Adjust time and temperature settings as per the requirements of your dish. Many air fryers include pre-programmed cooking modes, so you never have to choose time and temperature settings manually.

6. ***Cooking process:*** After setting the time and temperature, the cooking process starts automatically when the air fryer basket is closed back to its original position. The air fryer works its magic by circulating hot air all around the food basket to cook your delicious food faster and evenly.

7. ***Toss or shake the food basket:*** Toss or shake the food basket halfway during the cooking time. This makes sure that the dish cooks thoroughly from all sides.

8. ***Take Out the Food Basket:*** Once the countdown timer hits zero, use heatproof mitts or gloves to take out the food basket. Your tasty meal is now ready to be served.

Functions of Air Fryer

The Ninja air fryer is a multitasking air fryer that comes with various cooking functions. It not only allows you to air fry but also bake, grill, roast, and dehydrate your favourite food. Some of the Ninja air fryer functions include:

- *Air Fry:* Air frying is one of the healthiest ways to cook your favourite food by using minimal fats and oils. Using this function, you can cook your favourite food, such as French fries, chicken wings, onion rings, and more. It makes your chicken crispy on the outside and juicy on the inside.

- *Max Crisp:* This feature is one of the most effective when used with frozen food, such as French fries, onion rings, chicken fingers, chicken nuggets, and chicken pops. You may get extremely crisp exteriors for baked or fried foods by using the max crisp feature. Your frozen food will crisp up in a matter of minutes when you use this feature, which blasts very hot air around the food basket.

- *Air Roast:* Air fryers have an air roast feature that helps you cook meats, veggies, and other foods by circulating hot air around them. This makes it simple to get that roasted texture and even cook without using too much oil or fats.

- *Air Broil:* The air broil function in the Ninja air fryer enables you to prepare food in a way that resembles broiling. It utilises circulating air to cook the food, resulting in a crispy and caramelised texture. This feature is beneficial as it allows you to achieve an appearance without the need for oil or fats.

- *Bake:* The bake feature found in Ninja air fryers is specifically designed to fulfill your baking needs. It guarantees uniform and consistent heat distribution, creating the environment for all your baking ventures. So, whether you are making a cake, cookies, mouthwatering casseroles, or delectable pies, this function ensures optimal results every time.

- *Reheat:* Ninja air fryers come with a special reheat function. You can use this function to warm up already cooked food without making it soggy or too dry, unlike a microwave oven.

- *Dehydrate:* The Ninja air fryer is loaded with a special setting known as dehydrate, just for dehydrating your favourite food. It helps you slowly remove moisture from fruits, vegetables, and jerky and convert them into dried snacks. This feature is great for preserving food, so it lasts longer.

BREAKFAST RECIPES

Fruit Flapjack

INGREDIENTS: **SERVES: 4**   **COOK TIME: 20 minutes**

- Egg - 1
- Old-fashioned oats - 340 grams
- Baking powder - 1 1/2 tsp
- Maple syrup - 60 ml
- Blueberries - 150 grams
- Strawberries, sliced - 150 grams
- Milk - 355 ml
- Salt - 1/2 tsp
- Vanilla - 1/2 tsp

DIRECTIONS:

1. Spray a baking dish with cooking spray and set aside.
2. In a mixing bowl, mix oats, baking powder, and salt.
3. Add egg, vanilla, maple syrup, and milk and stir well. Add berries and stir well.
4. Pour the oat mixture into the baking dish. Place the baking dish into the air fryer basket.
5. Select Bake mode and cook at 190°C for 20 minutes.
6. Serve and enjoy.

PER SERVING: Calories 323, Carbs 65.84g, Fat 9.04g, Protein 13.92g

Broccoli Breakfast Bake

INGREDIENTS: **SERVES: 12**   **COOK TIME: 30 minutes**

- Eggs - 12
- Mozzarella cheese, shredded - 225 grams
- Broccoli florets, chopped - 280 grams
- Onion, diced - 1 medium
- Milk - 240 ml
- Pepper
- Salt

DIRECTIONS:

1. Lightly grease a 9 x 13-inch baking dish with oil and set aside.
2. In a large bowl, mix eggs, milk, pepper, and salt.
3. Add broccoli, cheese, and onion and mix well.
4. Pour the egg mixture into the prepared baking dish. Place the baking dish into the air fryer basket.
5. Select Bake mode and cook at 200°C for 30 minutes.
6. Slice and serve.

PER SERVING: Calories 168, Carbs 3.88g, Fat 10.35g, Protein 14.47g

Healthy Breakfast Bars

INGREDIENTS: **SERVES: 16** **COOK TIME: 30 minutes**

- Whole wheat flour - 65 grams
- Maple syrup - 60 ml
- Mashed banana - 60 ml
- Vanilla - 1 tsp
- Butter - 120 grams
- Cinnamon - 1 tsp
- Baking soda - 1 tsp
- Rolled oats - 180 grams
- Ground linseed - 2 tbsp
- Carrot, grated - 100 grams
- Milk - 180 ml

DIRECTIONS:

1. In a mixing bowl, whisk milk, maple syrup, carrot, butter, vanilla, mashed banana, and ground linseed.
2. Add oats, cinnamon, flour, and baking soda and mix until well combined.
3. Pour the mixture into the greased baking pan. Place the baking pan into the air fryer basket.
4. Select Bake mode and cook at 180°C for 30 minutes.
5. Slice and serve.

PER SERVING: Calories 121, Carbs 14.96g, Fat 7.43g, Protein 2.81g

Cheesy Hash Brown Cups

INGREDIENTS: **SERVES: 12** **COOK TIME: 30 minutes**

- Eggs - 8
- Hash browns - 565 grams
- Cheddar cheese, grated - 225 grams
- Milk - 2 tbsp
- Garlic powder - 1/4 tsp
- Ham, cubed - 150 grams
- Pepper
- Salt

DIRECTIONS:

1. In a bowl, whisk eggs with milk, pepper, and salt. Add cheese, ham, and hash browns and stir to combine.
2. Pour the egg mixture into the greased muffin pan. Place the muffin pan into the air fryer basket.
3. Select Bake mode and cook at 180°C for 30 minutes.
4. Serve and enjoy.

PER SERVING: Calories 389, Carbs 45.27g, Fat 14.18g, Protein 19.38g

Apple Breakfast Bake

INGREDIENTS: SERVES: 6 COOK TIME: 40 minutes

- Eggs - 3
- Apple, peel & dice - 1
- Cinnamon - 1 tsp
- Pecans, chopped - 50 grams
- Milk - 150 ml
- Pumpkin puree - 240 grams
- Pumpkin pie spice - 1 tsp
- Banana, mashed - 1
- Salt - 1/4 tsp

DIRECTIONS:

1. In a mixing bowl, whisk eggs, pumpkin pie spice, cinnamon, banana, milk, pumpkin puree, and salt until well combined.
2. Add apple and fold well. Pour the mixture into the greased baking pan. Sprinkle pecans on top.
3. Place the baking pan into the air fryer basket.
4. Select Bake mode and cook at 180°C for 40 minutes.
5. Slice and serve.

PER SERVING: Calories 253, Carbs 6.39g, Fat 21.34g, Protein 12g

Greek Spinach Egg Cups

INGREDIENTS: SERVES: 6 COOK TIME: 20 minutes

- Eggs - 6
- Feta cheese, crumbled - 75 grams
- Onion powder - 1/8 tsp
- Garlic powder - 1/8 tsp
- Spinach, chopped - 355 grams
- Pepper
- Salt

DIRECTIONS:

1. Lightly grease a 6-cup muffin pan with oil.
2. Divide spinach and cheese evenly into each muffin cup.
3. In a bowl, whisk eggs with pepper, garlic powder, onion powder, and salt.
4. Pour egg mixture into each cup. Place the muffin pan into the air fryer basket.
5. Select Bake mode and cook at 180°C for 20 minutes.
6. Serve and enjoy.

PER SERVING: Calories 156, Carbs 2.42g, Fat 11.44g, Protein 10.52g

Baked Egg Quiche

INGREDIENTS: **SERVES: 6** **COOK TIME: 55 minutes**

- Eggs - 8
- Cheddar cheese, shredded - 225 grams
- Ground Italian sausage - 450 grams
- Sour cream - 240 ml
- Ranch seasoning (a mix of parsley, dill weed, garlic powder, onion powder, basil and black pepper) - 3/4 tbsp
- Pepper
- Salt

DIRECTIONS:

1. Brown the ground sausage in a pan over medium heat. Drain well and set aside.
2. In a large bowl, whisk eggs with ranch seasoning, cream, pepper, and salt. Add sausage and cheese and stir well.
3. Pour the egg mixture into the greased baking dish. Place the baking dish into the air fryer basket.
4. Select Bake mode and cook at 180°C for 55 minutes.
5. Slice and serve.

PER SERVING: Calories 493, Carbs 5.89g, Fat 40.62g, Protein 24.27g

Breakfast Muffins

INGREDIENTS: **SERVES: 9** **COOK TIME: 15 minutes**

- Eggs - 2
- All-purpose flour - 90 grams
- Yellow cornmeal (or corn flour, different from the white powdery cornflour/cornstarch used to thicken gravy)- 150 grams
- Butter, melted - 85 grams
- Buttermilk - 355 ml
- Baking soda - 1/2 tsp
- Baking powder - 1 1/2 tsp
- Sugar - 1 tbsp
- Salt - 1/4 tsp

DIRECTIONS:

1. In a bowl, mix flour, sugar, cornmeal, baking soda, baking powder, and salt.
2. In a separate bowl, whisk eggs with buttermilk and butter.
3. Add egg mixture into the flour mixture and mix until well combined.
4. Spoon batter into the greased muffin pan. Place the muffin pan into the air fryer basket.
5. Select Air Fry mode and cook at 180°C for 15 minutes.
6. Serve and enjoy.

PER SERVING: Calories 219, Carbs 24.89g, Fat 10.59g, Protein 5.7g

Juicy Breakfast Meat Patties

INGREDIENTS: **SERVES: 6** **COOK TIME: 10 minutes**

- Ground pork - 450 grams
- Cayenne pepper - 1/8 tsp
- Thyme - 1/8 tsp
- Onion powder - 1/2 tsp
- Sage - 1/2 tsp
- Garlic powder - 1/2 tsp
- Fennel seeds, crushed - 1/2 tsp
- Pepper - 1/2 tsp
- Salt - 1 tsp

DIRECTIONS:

1. In a mixing bowl, mix meat and remaining ingredients until well combined. Cover and place in refrigerator for 2 hours.
2. Make equal shapes of patties from the meat mixture and place them into the air fryer basket. Spray patties using a cooking spray.
3. Select Air Fry mode and cook at 200°C for 10 minutes. Turn patties halfway through.
4. Serve and enjoy.

PER SERVING: Calories 229, Carbs 0.86g, Fat 15.75g, Protein 19.6g

Stuffed Bell Peppers

INGREDIENTS: **SERVES: 4** **COOK TIME: 22 minutes**

- Eggs - 4
- Bell peppers, cut ¼-inch off the top & remove seeds - 4
- Mozzarella cheese, shredded - 225 grams
- Spinach, chopped - 225 grams
- Mushrooms, sliced - 100 grams
- Pepper
- Salt

DIRECTIONS:

1. Add spinach and mushrooms to the air fryer pan and cook for 5 minutes at 180 C.
2. Stuff spinach and mushrooms in each pepper, then crack 1 egg into each pepper. Season with pepper and salt.
3. Place the stuffed peppers in the air fryer basket.
4. Select Air Fry mode and cook at 180°C for 15 minutes.
5. Sprinkle shredded cheese on top of peppers and cook for 2 minutes more or until cheese is melted.
6. Serve and enjoy.

PER SERVING: Calories 194, Carbs 7.65g, Fat 9.79g, Protein 19.31g

LUNCH RECIPES

Greek Baby Potatoes

INGREDIENTS: **SERVES: 4** **COOK TIME: 25 minutes**

- Baby potatoes, cut in half - 450 grams
- Thyme - 1 tsp
- Garlic cloves - 2
- Olive oil - 1 tbsp
- Parsley - 1 tbsp
- Feta cheese - 30 grams
- Pepper
- Salt

DIRECTIONS:

1. Toss potatoes with garlic, thyme, oil, pepper, and salt.
2. Add potatoes to the air fryer basket.
3. Select the Bake mode and cook at 200°C for 25 minutes.
4. Top with cheese and parsley, and serve.

PER SERVING: Calories 137, Carbs 21g, Fat 4g, Protein 3g

Creamy Turnip Gratin

INGREDIENTS: **SERVES: 6** **COOK TIME: 30 minutes**

- Turnip - 680 grams
- Butter - 40 grams
- Fresh chives - 4 tbsp
- Cheddar cheese - 225 grams
- Coconut milk - 300 ml
- Garlic - 1/2 tsp
- Onion - 1/2
- Pepper
- Salt

DIRECTIONS:

1. Lightly grease the baking dish with oil.
2. Arrange turnip and onion slices into the baking dish. Season with pepper and salt.
3. Pour milk over turnips and onion slices and sprinkle cheese on top.
4. Place the baking dish into the air fryer basket.
5. Select Bake mode and cook at 200°C for 30 minutes.
6. Sprinkle with chives. Serve and enjoy.

PER SERVING: Calories 276, Carbs 13g, Fat 21g, Protein 9g

Aubergine Gratin

SERVES: 6 **COOK TIME: 45 minutes**

INGREDIENTS:
- Aubergine - 900 grams
- Heavy cream - 180 ml
- Cheddar cheese - 85 grams
- Feta cheese - 150 grams
- Fried onion - 45 grams
- Olive oil - 2 tbsp
- Pepper
- Salt

DIRECTIONS:
1. Brush aubergine slices with oil and place into the baking dish. Season with pepper and salt.
2. Place the baking dish into the air fryer basket.
3. Select the Bake mode and cook at 200°C for 15 minutes.
4. Sprinkle fried onion over aubergine slices, then sprinkle with feta cheese and cheddar cheese. Pour cream over aubergine and cook for 30 minutes more.
5. Serve and enjoy.

PER SERVING: Calories 200, Carbs 11g, Fat 15g, Protein 5g

Greek Tilapia

SERVES: 2 **COOK TIME: 18 minutes**

INGREDIENTS:
- Tilapia fillets - 230 grams
- Garlic - 1 1/2 tbsp
- Fresh parsley - 80 grams
- Olive oil - 1 tsp
- Feta cheese - 60 grams
- Tomatoes – 160 grams
- Pepper
- Salt

DIRECTIONS:
1. In a bowl, mix tomatoes, parsley, garlic, feta, and olive oil.
2. Spray tilapia fillets with cooking spray and season with pepper and salt.
3. Place tilapia fillets into the baking dish and top with the tomato mixture. Place the baking dish into the air fryer basket.
4. Select Bake mode and cook at 200°C for 18 minutes.
5. Serve and enjoy.

PER SERVING: Calories 235, Carbs 8g, Fat 10g, Protein 28g

Quick Baked Cod

SERVES: 2 **COOK TIME:** 10 minutes

INGREDIENTS:
- Cod fillets - 450 grams
- Cayenne pepper - 1/8 tsp
- Fresh lemon juice - 1 tbsp
- Fresh parsley - 1 tbsp
- Olive oil - 1 1/2 tbsp
- Salt - 1/4 tsp

DIRECTIONS:
1. Place fish fillets into the baking dish.
2. Drizzle with oil and lemon juice and season with cayenne pepper and salt. Place the baking dish into the air fryer basket.
3. Select Bake mode and cook at 200°C for 10 minutes.
4. Garnish with parsley and serve.

PER SERVING: Calories 644, Carbs 150.1g, Fat 10.5g, Protein 2.4g

Lemon Pepper Basa

SERVES: 4 **COOK TIME:** 12 minutes

INGREDIENTS:
- Basa fish fillets - 4 fillets
- Fresh parsley - 2 tbsp
- Green onion - 60 grams
- Garlic powder - 1/2 tsp
- Lemon pepper seasoning - 1/4 tsp
- Fresh lemon juice - 60 ml
- Olive oil - 40 ml
- Pepper
- Salt

DIRECTIONS:
1. Arrange the fish fillets in a baking dish, drizzle oil and lemon juice, then sprinkle with the remaining ingredients.
2. Place the baking dish into the air fryer basket.
3. Select Bake mode and cook at 200°C for 12 minutes.
4. Serve and enjoy.

PER SERVING: Calories 274, Carbs 3g, Fat 19g, Protein 21g

Turkey Patties

SERVES: 4   **COOK TIME:** 20 minutes

INGREDIENTS:
- Ground turkey - 450 grams
- Egg - 1
- Almond flour - 120 grams
- Red pepper - 1/2 tsp
- Lemongrass - 1 tbsp
- Garlic cloves - 2
- Basil - 60 grams
- Scallions - 3 tbsp
- Fish sauce - 1 1/2 tbsp

DIRECTIONS:
1. Add all ingredients into a mixing bowl and mix until well combined.
2. Make equal shapes of patties from the meat mixture and place them into the air fryer basket.
3. Select Air Fry mode and cook at 190°C for 20 minutes. Turn patties halfway through.
4. Serve and enjoy.

PER SERVING: Calories 208, Carbs 1.42g, Fat 11g, Protein 25.9g

Herb Chicken Breasts

SERVES: 2   **COOK TIME:** 10 minutes

INGREDIENTS:
- Chicken breasts - 2
- Garlic - 2 tsp
- Dried thyme - 1 tsp
- Dried oregano - 1 tsp
- Dried basil - 1 tsp
- Pepper
- Salt

DIRECTIONS:
1. In a small bowl, mix garlic, basil, pepper, thyme, oregano, and salt and rub all over the chicken.
2. Place chicken into the air fryer basket.
3. Select Air Fry mode and cook at 200°C for 10 minutes.
4. Serve and enjoy.

PER SERVING: Calories 515, Carbs 3.8g, Fat 26.3g, Protein 61.7g

Marinated Chicken Breasts

INGREDIENTS: **SERVES: 4** **COOK TIME: 30 minutes**

- Chicken breasts - 450 grams
- Dill - 1/2 tsp
- Onion powder - 1 tsp
- Basil - 1/4 tsp
- Garlic cloves - 3
- Lemon juice - 1 tbsp
- Olive oil - 3 tbsp
- Oregano - 1/4 tsp
- Pepper - 1/4 tsp
- Salt - 1/2 tsp

DIRECTIONS:

1. Add all marinade ingredients into the large mixing bowl and mix well.
2. Add chicken into the marinade and coat well. Cover and place in the refrigerator overnight.
3. Place the crisper plate in the air fryer basket.
4. Arrange marinated chicken into the air fryer basket.
5. Select Bake mode and cook at 200°C for 30 minutes.
6. Serve and enjoy.

PER SERVING: Calories 293, Carbs 1.98g, Fat 20.5g, Protein 23.7g

Turkey Spinach Patties

INGREDIENTS: **SERVES: 4** **COOK TIME: 22 minutes**

- Ground turkey - 450 grams
- Spinach - 300 grams
- Italian seasoning - 1 tsp
- Garlic paste - 1 tbsp
- Feta cheese - 110 grams
- Olive oil - 1 tbsp
- Pepper
- Salt

DIRECTIONS:

1. Add all ingredients into the bowl and mix until well combined.
2. Make patties from the meat mixture and place them into the air fryer basket.
3. Select Air Fry mode and cook at 200°C for 22 minutes. Turn patties halfway through.
4. Serve and enjoy.

PER SERVING: Calories 285, Carbs 3.2g, Fat 18.5g, Protein 26.6g

APPETIZERS & SIDE DISHES

Perfect Garlic Bread

INGREDIENTS: **SERVES: 6**   **COOK TIME: 5 minutes**

- French loaf, sliced - 1 (approximately 400 grams)
- Fresh parsley, chopped - 60 grams
- Parmesan cheese, grated - 115 grams
- Garlic cloves, minced - 4 cloves
- Butter, unsalted - 115 grams
- Pepper
- Salt

DIRECTIONS:

1. In a small bowl, mix butter, parsley, parmesan cheese, garlic, pepper, and salt.
2. Spread butter mixture onto bread slices.
3. Arrange the bread slices into an air fryer basket in a single layer.
4. Select Air Fry mode and cook at 180°C for 5 minutes.
5. Serve and enjoy.

PER SERVING: Calories 196, Carbs 5.32g, Fat 18.3g, Protein 3.5g

Healthy & Tasty Butternut Squash

INGREDIENTS: **SERVES: 4**   **COOK TIME: 12 minutes**

- Butternut squash, peeled & cubed - 450 grams
- Smoked paprika - 1 tsp
- Garlic powder - 1 tsp
- Olive oil - 15 ml
- Pepper
- Salt

DIRECTIONS:

1. Add butternut squash cubes and remaining ingredients into the mixing bowl and toss to coat.
2. Add the squash cubes to the air fryer basket.
3. Select Air Fry mode and cook at 200°C for 12 minutes.
4. Serve and enjoy.

PER SERVING: Calories 381, Carbs 7.6g, Fat 32.2g, Protein 17.9g

Garlic Parmesan Cauliflower

INGREDIENTS: **SERVES: 4** **COOK TIME: 15 minutes**

- Cauliflower head, cut into florets - 220 grams
- Parmesan cheese, shredded - 80 grams
- Garlic powder - 1/2 tsp
- Olive oil - 30 ml
- Paprika - 1/4 tsp
- Pepper
- Salt

DIRECTIONS:

1. In a bowl, toss cauliflower florets with garlic powder, oil, paprika, pepper, and salt until well coated.
2. Add cauliflower florets into the air fryer basket and spread evenly.
3. Select Air Fry mode and cook at 200°C for 12 minutes.
4. Sprinkle parmesan cheese over cauliflower florets and cook for 3 minutes more.
5. Serve and enjoy.

PER SERVING: Calories 109, Carbs 4.23g, Fat 9.18g, Protein 3.29g

Crispy Broccoli Tots

INGREDIENTS: **SERVES: 6** **COOK TIME: 10 minutes**

- Egg - 1
- Broccoli, roasted & minced - 180 grams
- Breadcrumbs - 60 grams
- Mustard powder - 1/2 tsp
- Onion powder - 1/2 tsp
- Cheddar cheese, shredded - 60 grams
- Pepper
- Salt

DIRECTIONS:

1. Line the air fryer basket with parchment paper.
2. In a mixing bowl, mix broccoli, egg, breadcrumbs, mustard powder, onion powder, cheddar cheese, pepper, and salt until well combined.
3. Make equal shapes of tots from the broccoli mixture and place them into the air fryer basket.
4. Select Air Fry mode and cook at 190°C for 10 minutes.
5. Serve and enjoy.

PER SERVING: Calories 27, Carbs 1.3g, Fat 1.68g, Protein 1.95g

Banana Chips

INGREDIENTS: **SERVES: 4** **COOK TIME: 12 hours**

- Raw bananas, peeled & sliced evenly - 2 (approximately 300 grams)
- Lemon juice - 120 ml
- Water – 2 cups

DIRECTIONS:

1. In a mixing bowl, add lemon juice, 2 cups of water, and slice bananas. Allow to soak for 5 minutes. Remove banana slices from the lemon water.
2. Arrange banana slices into the air fryer basket in a single layer. Place the crisper plate in the air fryer basket and arrange the remaining banana slices on the crisper plate.
3. Select Dehydrate mode and cook at 60°C for 10 hours. Flip banana slices and cook for 2 hours more.
4. Serve and enjoy.

PER SERVING: Calories 0.07, Carbs 2.1g, Fat 0.07g, Protein 0.11g

Brussels Sprout Chips

INGREDIENTS: **SERVES: 4** **COOK TIME: 10 hours**

- Brussels sprouts, cut the stem, and separate leaves - 450 grams
- Soy sauce - 1 tsp
- Sriracha - 1 tbsp
- Pinch of salt

DIRECTIONS:

1. In a mixing bowl, toss Brussels sprouts with sriracha, soy sauce, and salt.
2. Arrange Brussels sprouts into the air fryer basket in a single layer. Place the crisper plate in the air fryer basket and arrange the remaining Brussels sprouts on the crisper plate.
3. Select Dehydrate mode and cook at 45°C for 10 hours.
4. Serve and enjoy.

PER SERVING: Calories 53, Carbs 10.48g, Fat 0.58g, Protein 3.93g

Onion Dip

SERVES: 8 **COOK TIME: 40 minutes**

INGREDIENTS:
- Onions, chopped - 300 grams
- Mozzarella cheese, shredded - 115 grams
- Cheddar cheese, shredded - 115 grams
- Mayonnaise - 360 ml
- Garlic powder - 1/2 tsp
- Swiss cheese, shredded - 115 grams
- Pepper
- Salt

DIRECTIONS:
1. Spray a baking dish with cooking spray and set aside.
2. Add all ingredients into the mixing bowl and mix until well combined.
3. Pour the mixture into the prepared baking dish. Place the baking dish into the air fryer basket.
4. Select Bake mode and cook at 180°C for 40 minutes.
5. Serve and enjoy.

PER SERVING: Calories 270, Carbs 5.81g, Fat 21.22g, Protein 14.19g

Baked Chicken Meatballs

SERVES: 6 **COOK TIME: 30 minutes**

INGREDIENTS:
- Egg - 1
- Breadcrumbs - 60 grams
- Ground chicken - 450 grams
- Ground ginger - 1/2 tsp
- Garlic powder - 1 tsp
- Pepper - 1/4 tsp
- Salt - 1 tsp

DIRECTIONS:
1. Add all ingredients into the mixing bowl and mix until well combined.
2. Place the crisper plate in the air fryer basket.
3. Make balls from the meat mixture and place them into the air fryer basket.
4. Select Bake mode and cook at 200°C for 30 minutes.
5. Serve and enjoy.

PER SERVING: Calories 187, Carbs 0.83g, Fat 13.01g, Protein 15.69g

Crispy Potato Fries

INGREDIENTS: **SERVES: 2**   **COOK TIME: 18 minutes**

- Potato, cut into fries shape - 450 grams
- Garlic granules - 1 tbsp
- Olive oil - 15 ml
- Pepper
- Salt

DIRECTIONS:

1. In a mixing bowl, toss potato fries with garlic granules, oil, pepper, and salt until well coated.
2. Place the crisper plate in the air fryer basket.
3. Select Max Crisp mode and cook for 18 minutes. Shake the basket after 10 minutes.
4. Serve and enjoy.

PER SERVING: Calories 250, Carbs 43.16g, Fat 7.02g, Protein 5.3g

Roasted Cashews

INGREDIENTS: **SERVES: 8**   **COOK TIME: 8 minutes**

- Cashews - 450 grams
- Chili powder - 1/2 tsp
- Rosemary - 2 tbsp
- Worcestershire sauce - 10 ml
- Brown sugar - 2 tsp
- Mustard powder - 1/2 tsp
- Butter, melted - 15 grams

DIRECTIONS:

1. Add cashews and remaining ingredients into the mixing bowl and toss well to coat.
2. Add cashews to the air fryer basket.
3. Select Air Fry mode and cook at 150°C for 8 minutes. Stir cashews halfway through.
4. Serve and enjoy.

PER SERVING: Calories 331, Carbs 18.07g, Fat 26.36g, Protein 10.4g

FISH & SEAFOOD RECIPES

Perfect Salmon Patties

INGREDIENTS: **SERVES: 4**   **COOK TIME: 12 minutes**

- Egg - 1
- Salmon, drained - 400 grams
- Lemon pepper seasoning - 1/2 tsp
- Dijon mustard - 2 tsp
- Mayonnaise - 2 tbsp
- Italian breadcrumbs - 40 grams

DIRECTIONS:

1. Add salmon and remaining ingredients into the mixing bowl and mix until well combined.
2. Make equal shapes of patties from the salmon mixture and spray each side with cooking spray.
3. Place patties into the air fryer basket.
4. Select Air Fry mode and cook at 200°C for 12 minutes. Turn patties halfway through.
5. Serve and enjoy.

PER SERVING: Calories 224, Carbs 1.91g, Fat 12.53g, Protein 24.21g

Simple & Quick Salmon

INGREDIENTS: **SERVES: 4**   **COOK TIME: 6 minutes**

- Salmon fillets - 2 (approximately 300 grams)
- Olive oil - 15 ml
- Smoked paprika - 1/4 tsp
- Garlic powder - 1/4 tsp
- Brown sugar - 1 tbsp
- 1/8 tsp pepper
- ¼ tsp salt

DIRECTIONS:

1. In a small bowl, mix paprika, garlic powder, brown sugar, pepper, and salt.
2. Brush salmon fillets with and rub with spice mixture.
3. Arrange salmon fillets into the air fryer basket. Select Air Fry mode and cook at 200°C for 6 minutes.
4. Serve and enjoy.

PER SERVING: Calories 39, Carbs 2.36g, Fat 3.4g, Protein 0.08g

Crab Patties

SERVES: 6 **COOK TIME:** 30 minutes

INGREDIENTS:
- Lump crab meat - 450 grams
- Mashed avocado - 150 grams
- Celery, diced - 60 grams
- Onion, diced - 60 grams
- Crushed crackers - 100 grams
- Old bay seasoning - 1 tsp
- Brown mustard - 1 tsp

DIRECTIONS:
1. Add crab meat and remaining ingredients into the mixing bowl and mix until well combined.
2. Place the crisper plate in the air fryer basket
3. Make patties from the mixture and place them into the air fryer basket.
4. Select Bake mode and cook at 180°C for 30 minutes.
5. Serve and enjoy.

PER SERVING: Calories 270, Carbs 31.42g, Fat 4.89g, Protein 29.3g

Quick Scallop Gratin

SERVES: 4 **COOK TIME:** 8 minutes

INGREDIENTS:
- Sea scallops - 680 grams
- Parmesan cheese, shaved - 60 grams
- Tarragon, chopped - 15 grams
- White wine - 60 ml
- Cream cheese softened - 60 grams
- Lemon juice – 1
- Salt and pepper to taste

DIRECTIONS:
1. Add scallops to the baking dish.
2. In a bowl, whisk white wine, tarragon, Parmesan cheese, lemon juice, cream cheese, pepper, and salt and pour over scallops.
3. Place the baking dish in the air fryer basket.
4. Select Bake mode and cook at 200°C for 8 minutes.
5. Serve and enjoy.

PER SERVING: Calories 230, Carbs 3.67g, Fat 14.62g, Protein 42.24g

Baked Dijon Salmon

INGREDIENTS: **SERVES: 4** **COOK TIME: 12 minutes**

- Salmon fillets - 4 (approximately 600 grams)
- Ground Dijon mustard - 2 tbsp
- Maple syrup - 45 ml

DIRECTIONS:

1. Place the crisper plate in the air fryer basket
2. Arrange salmon fillets into the air fryer basket.
3. Mix Dijon mustard and maple syrup and brush over salmon fillets.
4. Select Bake mode and cook at 200°C for 12 minutes.
5. Serve and enjoy.

PER SERVING: Calories 55, Carbs 10.94g, Fat 1.15g, Protein 26.1g

Healthy Baked Cod

INGREDIENTS: **SERVES: 2** **COOK TIME: 10 minutes**

- Cod fillets - 450 grams
- Fresh lemon juice - 15 ml
- Olive oil - 20 ml
- Fresh parsley, chopped - 15 grams
- Cayenne pepper - 1/8 tsp
- Salt - 1/4 tsp

DIRECTIONS:

1. Place fish fillets in the baking dish.
2. Drizzle with lemon juice and oil and season with cayenne pepper and salt.
3. Select Bake mode and cook at 200°C for 10 minutes.
4. Garnish with parsley and serve.

PER SERVING: Calories 750, Carbs 21.12g, Fat 51.02g, Protein 52.26g

Crab Patties

SERVES: 6 **COOK TIME: 30 minutes**

INGREDIENTS:
- Lump crab meat - 450 grams
- Mashed avocado - 150 grams
- Celery, diced - 60 grams
- Onion, diced - 60 grams
- Crushed crackers - 100 grams
- Old bay seasoning - 1 tsp
- Brown mustard - 1 tsp

DIRECTIONS:
1. Add crab meat and remaining ingredients into the mixing bowl and mix until well combined.
2. Place the crisper plate in the air fryer basket
3. Make patties from the mixture and place them into the air fryer basket.
4. Select Bake mode and cook at 180°C for 30 minutes.
5. Serve and enjoy.

PER SERVING: Calories 270, Carbs 31.42g, Fat 4.89g, Protein 29.3g

Quick Scallop Gratin

SERVES: 4 **COOK TIME: 8 minutes**

INGREDIENTS:
- Sea scallops - 680 grams
- Parmesan cheese, shaved - 60 grams
- Tarragon, chopped - 15 grams
- White wine - 60 ml
- Cream cheese softened - 60 grams
- Lemon juice – 1
- Salt and pepper to taste

DIRECTIONS:
1. Add scallops to the baking dish.
2. In a bowl, whisk white wine, tarragon, Parmesan cheese, lemon juice, cream cheese, pepper, and salt and pour over scallops.
3. Place the baking dish in the air fryer basket.
4. Select Bake mode and cook at 200°C for 8 minutes.
5. Serve and enjoy.

PER SERVING: Calories 230, Carbs 3.67g, Fat 14.62g, Protein 42.24g

Baked Dijon Salmon

INGREDIENTS: **SERVES: 4**   **COOK TIME: 12 minutes**

- Salmon fillets - 4 (approximately 600 grams)
- Ground Dijon mustard - 2 tbsp
- Maple syrup - 45 ml

DIRECTIONS:

1. Place the crisper plate in the air fryer basket
2. Arrange salmon fillets into the air fryer basket.
3. Mix Dijon mustard and maple syrup and brush over salmon fillets.
4. Select Bake mode and cook at 200°C for 12 minutes.
5. Serve and enjoy.

PER SERVING: Calories 55, Carbs 10.94g, Fat 1.15g, Protein 26.1g

Healthy Baked Cod

INGREDIENTS: **SERVES: 2**   **COOK TIME: 10 minutes**

- Cod fillets - 450 grams
- Fresh lemon juice - 15 ml
- Olive oil - 20 ml
- Fresh parsley, chopped - 15 grams
- Cayenne pepper - 1/8 tsp
- Salt - 1/4 tsp

DIRECTIONS:

1. Place fish fillets in the baking dish.
2. Drizzle with lemon juice and oil and season with cayenne pepper and salt.
3. Select Bake mode and cook at 200°C for 10 minutes.
4. Garnish with parsley and serve.

PER SERVING: Calories 750, Carbs 21.12g, Fat 51.02g, Protein 52.26g

Shrimp Casserole

INGREDIENTS: **SERVES:** 4   **COOK TIME:** 12 minutes

- Shrimp, peeled and deveined - 450 grams
- Garlic, minced - 1 tbsp
- Fresh parsley, chopped - 30 grams
- Breadcrumbs - 60 grams
- Butter, melted - 60 grams
- White wine - 30 ml
- Pepper
- Salt

DIRECTIONS:

1. Add shrimp into the mixing bowl. Pour all remaining ingredients over the shrimp and toss well.
2. Pour the shrimp mixture into the baking dish. Place the baking dish into the air fryer basket.
3. Select Bake mode and cook at 165°C for 12 minutes.
4. Serve and enjoy.

PER SERVING: Calories 207, Carbs 1.98g, Fat 12.14g, Protein 23.37g

Rosemary Garlic Shrimp

INGREDIENTS: **SERVES:** 4   **COOK TIME:** 10 minutes

- Shrimp, peeled and deveined - 450 grams
- Butter, melted - 15 grams
- Fresh rosemary, chopped - 1 tsp
- Garlic, minced - 1 tbsp
- Pepper
- Salt

DIRECTIONS:

1. Add shrimp and remaining ingredients in a large bowl and toss well.
2. Pour the shrimp mixture into the baking dish. Place the baking dish into the air fryer basket.
3. Select Bake mode and cook at 200°C for 10 minutes.
4. Serve and enjoy.

PER SERVING: Calories 130, Carbs 1.82g, Fat 3.5g, Protein 23.19g

Quick & Spicy Shrimp

INGREDIENTS: **SERVES: 4** **COOK TIME: 8 minutes**

- Shrimp, peeled and deveined - 680 grams
- Ground cumin - 1/4 tsp
- Chipotle in adobo - 10 ml
- Olive oil - 30 ml
- Lime juice - 60 ml

DIRECTIONS:

1. Add shrimp, cumin, oil, lime juice, and chipotle into the mixing bowl and mix well. Cover and place in the refrigerator for 30 minutes.
2. Add marinated shrimp into the air fryer basket.
3. Select Air Fry mode and cook at 180°C for 8 minutes. Stir halfway through.
4. Serve and enjoy.

PER SERVING: Calories 236, Carbs 4.69g, Fat 9.26g, Protein 35.56g

Greek Salmon

INGREDIENTS: **SERVES: 4** **COOK TIME: 20 minutes**

- Salmon fillets - 4 (approximately 600 grams)
- Onion, chopped - 1 (approximately 150 grams)
- Feta cheese, crumbled - 120 grams
- Basil pesto - 120 ml
- Grape tomatoes, halved - 400 grams

DIRECTIONS:

1. Spray a baking dish with cooking spray and set aside.
2. Place salmon fillets in a baking dish and top with pesto, tomatoes, onion, and cheese.
3. Place the baking dish into the air fryer basket.
4. Select Bake mode and cook at 180°C for 20 minutes.
5. Serve and enjoy.

PER SERVING: Calories 113, Carbs 17.08g, Fat 4.16g, Protein 3.6g

POULTRY RECIPES

Juicy Chicken Breasts

INGREDIENTS: **SERVES: 4**   **COOK TIME: 18 minutes**

- Chicken breast, skinless & boneless - 450 grams
- Garlic powder - 1/4 tsp
- Onion powder - 1/4 tsp
- Parsley flakes - 1/2 tsp
- Paprika - 1/2 tsp
- Olive oil - 15 ml
- Pepper
- Salt

DIRECTIONS:

1. Add chicken and remaining ingredients into the zip-lock bag, seal the bag, and shake well to coat the chicken. Place in refrigerator for overnight to marinate.
2. Arrange marinated chicken into the air fryer basket.
3. Select Air Fry mode and cook at 180°C for 18 minutes. Flip the chicken halfway through.
4. Serve and enjoy.

PER SERVING: Calories 231, Carbs 1.5g, Fat 13.93g, Protein 23.96g

Southwest Chicken Breasts

INGREDIENTS: **SERVES: 4**   **COOK TIME: 20 minutes**

- Chicken breasts, boneless - 4 (approximately 680 grams)
- Garlic powder - 1/4 tsp
- Ground cumin - 1/2 tsp
- Chili powder - 3/4 tsp
- Olive oil - 15 ml
- Fresh lime juice - 30 ml
- Salt - 1/4 tsp

DIRECTIONS:

1. In a mixing bowl, add chicken, garlic powder, cumin, chili powder, olive oil, lime juice, and salt and mix until well coated.
2. Arrange the chicken into the air fryer basket. Select Air Fry mode and cook at 190°C for 20 minutes. Turn the chicken halfway through.
3. Serve and enjoy.

PER SERVING: Calories 534, Carbs 1.15g, Fat 30.34g, Protein 60.65g

Meatballs

SERVES: 4 **COOK TIME: 12 minutes**

INGREDIENTS:

- Egg - 1
- Ground turkey - 450 grams
- Parmesan cheese, grated - 60 grams
- Italian breadcrumbs - 120 grams
- Onion, grated - 30 grams
- Worcestershire sauce - 10 ml
- Italian seasoning - 1 tsp
- Salt - 1/4 tsp

DIRECTIONS:

1. Add ground turkey and remaining ingredients into the mixing bowl and mix until well combined.
2. Make equal shapes of balls from the meat mixture and place them into the air fryer basket.
3. Select Air Fry mode and cook at 180°C for 12 minutes.
4. Serve and enjoy.

PER SERVING: Calories 614, Carbs 3.04, Fat 54.57g, Protein 25.96g

Juicy Turkey Patties

SERVES: 4 **COOK TIME: 14 minutes**

INGREDIENTS:

- Egg yolk - 1
- Ground turkey - 450 grams
- Worcestershire sauce - 1 tbsp
- Onion powder - 1 tsp
- Italian breadcrumbs - 45 grams
- Olive oil - 15 ml
- BBQ sauce - 60 ml
- Pepper
- Salt

DIRECTIONS:

1. In a mixing bowl, mix ground turkey, egg yolk, Worcestershire sauce, onion powder, breadcrumbs, oil, pepper, and salt until well combined.
2. Make equal shapes of patties from the meat mixture and place them into the air fryer basket. Brush patties with half BBQ sauce.
3. Select Air Fry mode and cook at 180°C for 6 minutes.
4. Turn patties, brush with remaining BBQ sauce, and cook for 8 minutes more.
5. Serve and enjoy.

PER SERVING: Calories 601, Carbs 2.69g, Fat 54.95g, Protein 22.6g

Chicken Jerky

SERVES: 4   **COOK TIME:** 7 hours

INGREDIENTS:

- Chicken tenders, boneless & cut into 1/4-inch slices - 680 grams
- Soy sauce - 120 ml
- Ground ginger - 1/4 tsp
- Black pepper - 1/4 tsp
- Garlic powder - 1/2 tsp
- Lemon juice - 1 tsp

DIRECTIONS:

1. Mix all ingredients except chicken into the large mixing bowl. Add chicken slices and mix well, cover, and place in the refrigerator for 1 hour.
2. Arrange chicken slices into the air fryer basket in a single layer. Place the crisper plate in the air fryer basket and arrange the remaining chicken slices on the crisper plate.
3. Select Dehydrate mode and cook at 60°C for 7 hours.
4. Serve and enjoy.

PER SERVING: Calories 284, Carbs 8.51g, Fat 10.38g, Protein 36.95g

Baked Meatballs

SERVES: 6   **COOK TIME:** 25 minutes

INGREDIENTS:

- Egg - 1
- Ground chicken - 450 grams
- Olive oil - 30 ml
- Parsley, chopped - 1 tbsp
- Breadcrumbs - 60 grams
- Red pepper flakes - 1/4 tsp
- Pepper - 1/4 tsp
- Dried oregano - 1/2 tsp
- Dried onion flakes - 1/2 tsp
- Garlic clove, minced - 1
- Parmesan cheese, grated - 60 grams
- Sea salt - 1/2 tsp

DIRECTIONS:

1. Add all ingredients into the mixing bowl and mix until well combined.
2. Place the crisper plate in the air fryer basket.
3. Make balls from the meat mixture and place them into the air fryer basket.
4. Select Bake mode and cook at 200°C for 25 minutes.
5. Serve and enjoy.

PER SERVING: Calories 262, Carbs 1.94g, Fat 19.83g, Protein 18.04g

Balsamic Chicken

INGREDIENTS: **SERVES: 4**   **COOK TIME: 25 minutes**

- Chicken breasts, boneless & skinless - 4 (approximately 600 grams)
- Dried oregano - 2 tsp
- Garlic clove, minced - 2
- Balsamic vinegar - 120 ml
- Soy sauce - 30 ml
- Olive oil - 60 ml
- Pepper - 1/4 tsp
- Salt - 1/4 tsp

DIRECTIONS:

1. Place chicken into the baking dish.
2. Mix the remaining ingredients and pour over the chicken. Place the baking dish into the air fryer basket.
3. Select Bake mode and cook at 200°C for 25 minutes.
4. Serve and enjoy.

PER SERVING: Calories 674, Carbs 8.52g, Fat 41.8g, Protein 61.39g

Creamy Chicken Breasts

INGREDIENTS: **SERVES: 4**   **COOK TIME: 45 minutes**

- Chicken breasts, skinless, boneless & cut into chunks - 4 (approximately 600 grams)
- Mayonnaise - 240 ml
- Parmesan cheese, shredded - 115 grams
- Garlic powder - 1 tsp
- Salt and pepper

DIRECTIONS:

1. Add chicken to the large bowl. Add buttermilk and soak overnight.
2. Add marinated chicken to the 9 x 13-inch baking dish.
3. Mix mayonnaise, 1/2 cup Parmesan cheese, garlic powder, pepper, and salt and pour over chicken.
4. Sprinkle the remaining cheese on top of the chicken. Place the baking dish in the air fryer basket.
5. Select Bake mode and cook at 190°C for 45 minutes.
6. Serve and enjoy.

PER SERVING: Calories 804, Carbs 6.94g, Fat 52.89g, Protein 71.49g

Cheesy Chicken Broccoli

INGREDIENTS: **SERVES: 4**   **COOK TIME: 30 minutes**

- Chicken breasts, skinless and boneless - 4 (approximately 600 grams)
- Broccoli florets, blanched and chopped - 200 grams
- Mozzarella cheese, shredded - 80 grams
- Bacon slices, cooked and chopped - 4
- Ranch dressing (you could use a blue cheese dressing or Caesar salad dressing if you can't get hold of this) - 120 ml
- Cheddar cheese, shredded - 115 grams

DIRECTIONS:

1. Add chicken to a 13 x 9-inch casserole dish. Top with broccoli and bacon.
2. Pour ranch dressing over chicken and top with cheddar cheese and mozzarella cheese. Place the casserole dish into the air fryer basket.
3. Select Bake mode and cook at 190°C for 30 minutes.
4. Serve and enjoy.

PER SERVING: Calories 748, Carbs 2.83g, Fat 4.9g, Protein 25.4g

Baked Chicken Thighs

INGREDIENTS: **SERVES: 6**   **COOK TIME: 35 minutes**

- Chicken thighs - 6 (approximately 900 grams)
- Olive oil - 15 ml
- Basil - 1/2 tsp
- Oregano - 1/2 tsp
- Pepper - 1/2 tsp
- Garlic powder - 1 tsp
- Onion powder - 1 tsp
- Salt - 1/2 tsp

DIRECTIONS:

1. Brush chicken with oil.
2. In a small bowl, mix basil, oregano, pepper, garlic powder, onion powder, and salt and rub all over the chicken.
3. Place the crisper plate in the air fryer basket.
4. Arrange the chicken into the air fryer basket.
5. Select Bake mode and cook at 200°C for 35 minutes.
6. Serve and enjoy.

PER SERVING: Calories 451, Carbs 1.59g, Fat 34.33g, Protein 32.09g

Spiced Chicken Wings

INGREDIENTS: **SERVES: 6** **COOK TIME: 16 minutes**

- Chicken wings washed & pat dry - 725 grams
- Chili powder - 1 tbsp
- Paprika - 1 tbsp
- Cayenne pepper - 1 tsp
- Garlic salt - 1 tbsp
- Brown sugar - 110 grams
- Pepper - 1 tsp
- Garlic powder - 2 tbsp
- Salt - 1 tbsp

DIRECTIONS:

1. In a small bowl, mix garlic powder, chili powder, paprika, garlic salt, brown sugar, pepper, cayenne, and salt.
2. Add chicken wings and spice mixture into the mixing bowl and mix until chicken wings are well coated.
3. Arrange chicken wings in the air fryer basket.
4. Select Air Fry mode and cook at 200°C for 16 minutes. Flip chicken wings halfway through.
5. Serve and enjoy.

PER SERVING: Calories 169, Carbs 17.18g, Fat 3.19g, Protein 18.08g

Cheesy Chicken Patties

INGREDIENTS: **SERVES: 4** **COOK TIME: 25 minutes**

- Egg, lightly beaten - 1
- Ground chicken - 454 grams
- Cheddar cheese, grated - 115 grams
- Carrot, grated - 115 grams
- Cauliflower, grated - 115 grams
- Garlic, minced - 1 tsp
- Onion, minced - 115 grams
- Breadcrumbs - 180 grams

DIRECTIONS:

1. Add all ingredients into the bowl and mix until well combined.
2. Place the crisper plate in the air fryer basket.
3. Make small patties from the meat mixture and place them into the air fryer basket.
4. Select Bake mode and cook at 200°C for 25 minutes.
5. Serve and enjoy.

PER SERVING: Calories 302, Carbs 7.04g, Fat 19.35g, Protein 24.17g

Tasty Chicken Wings

SERVES: 4 **COOK TIME: 30 minutes**

INGREDIENTS:
- Chicken wings - 900 grams
- Onion powder - 2 tbsp
- Garlic powder - 2 tbsp
- Dried dill spice - 1 tbsp
- Chipotle spice - 1 tbsp
- Pepper
- Salt

DIRECTIONS:
1. Toss chicken wings and remaining ingredients into the mixing bowl and toss well.
2. Place the crisper plate in the air fryer basket.
3. Arrange chicken wings into the air fryer basket.
4. Select Bake mode and cook at 200°C for 30 minutes. Flip chicken wings halfway through.
5. Serve and enjoy.

PER SERVING: Calories 323, Carbs 8.24g, Fat 8.31g, Protein 51.44g

Turkey Meatballs

SERVES: 6 **COOK TIME: 20 minutes**

INGREDIENTS:
- Egg - 1
- Ground turkey - 680 grams
- Almond flour - 80 grams
- Italian seasoning - 2 tbsp
- Fresh parsley, chopped - 240 grams
- Pepper
- Salt

DIRECTIONS:
1. Add all ingredients into the mixing bowl and mix until well combined.
2. Place the crisper plate in the air fryer basket.
3. Make small balls from the meat mixture and place them into the air fryer basket.
4. Select bake mode and cook at 200 C for 20 minutes.
5. Serve and enjoy.

PER SERVING: Calories 584, Carbs 3.18g, Fat 52.14g, Protein 23.66g

Cajun Herb Chicken Thighs

INGREDIENTS: **SERVES: 4** **COOK TIME: 25 minutes**

- Chicken thighs, boneless - 4 (approximately 600 grams)
- Cajun seasoning - 1/2 tsp
- Dried mixed herbs - 1 tsp
- Paprika - 1 tsp
- Parmesan cheese, grated - 30 grams
- Flour – 2.5 tbsp

DIRECTIONS:

1. In a bowl, mix almond flour, mixed herbs, cheese, paprika, and Cajun seasoning.
2. Spray chicken thighs with cooking spray.
3. Coat chicken with almond flour mixture and place in the air fryer basket.
4. Select Air Fry mode and cook at 200°C for 25 minutes. Turn the chicken halfway through.
5. Serve and enjoy.

PER SERVING: Calories 446, Carbs 1.54g, Fat 33.23g, Protein 33.07g

Juicy Turkey Patties

INGREDIENTS: **SERVES: 8** **COOK TIME: 25 minutes**

- Egg, lightly beaten - 1
- Ground turkey - 450 grams
- Coriander, chopped – 1.5 tbsp
- Italian seasoning - 1 tsp
- Lemon juice - 30 ml
- Garlic, minced - 1/2 tsp
- Breadcrumbs - 80 grams
- Pepper
- Salt

DIRECTIONS:

1. Add all ingredients into the mixing bowl and mix until well combined.
2. Place the crisper plate in the air fryer basket.
3. Make patties from the meat mixture and place them into the air fryer basket.
4. Select Bake mode and cook at 200°C for 25 minutes.
5. Serve and enjoy.

PER SERVING: Calories 292, Carbs 1.29g, Fat 26.27g, Protein 11.89g

Spiced Chicken Thighs

INGREDIENTS: **SERVES: 8**   **COOK TIME: 25 minutes**

- Chicken thigh, skinless and boneless - 1350 grams
- Cinnamon - 1 tbsp
- Ground nutmeg - 1/2 tsp
- Coriander powder - 1 tbsp
- Olive oil - 45 ml
- Cayenne - 1 tbsp
- Pepper
- Salt

DIRECTIONS:

1. In a small bowl, mix oil, cinnamon, coriander powder, nutmeg, pepper, and salt.
2. Rub spice mixture all over the chicken.
3. Place chicken in the air fryer basket.
4. Select Air Fry mode and cook at 150°C for 20 minutes.
5. Serve and enjoy.

PER SERVING: Calories 428, Carbs 2.19g, Fat 33.5g, Protein 28.34g

Greek Chicken Meatballs

INGREDIENTS: **SERVES: 6**   **COOK TIME: 10 minutes**

- Eggs - 2
- Ground chicken breast - 900 grams
- Ricotta cheese - 120 grams
- Fresh parsley, chopped - 60 grams
- Breadcrumbs - 120 grams
- Pepper
- Salt

DIRECTIONS:

1. Add all ingredients into the large mixing bowl and mix until well combined.
2. Make small balls from the meat mixture and place them in an air fryer basket.
3. Select air fry mode and cook at 190 C for 10 minutes.
4. Serve and enjoy.

PER SERVING: Calories 343, Carbs 1.83g, Fat 19.92g, Protein 37.07g

Jalapeno Chicken Meatballs

INGREDIENTS: **SERVES: 8** **COOK TIME: 10 minutes**

- Ground chicken - 900 grams
- Breadcrumbs - 45 grams
- Fresh coriander, chopped - 60 grams
- Scallions, sliced - 60 grams
- Jalapeno chili peppers, chopped - 2
- Ginger, grated - 2 tsp
- Garlic, crushed - 1 tsp
- Ground coriander - 1 tbsp
- Fish sauce - 15 ml
- Pepper
- Salt

DIRECTIONS:

1. Add chicken and remaining ingredients into the bowl and mix until well combined.
2. Place the crisper plate in the air fryer basket.
3. Make small balls from the mixture and place them into the air fryer basket.
4. Select Bake mode and cook at 200°C for 10 minutes.
5. Serve and enjoy.

PER SERVING: Calories 253, Carbs 2.14g, Fat 17.13g, Protein 21.65g

Greek Chicken Breast

INGREDIENTS: **SERVES: 8** **COOK TIME: 45 minutes**

- Chicken breasts, skinless and boneless - 8 (approximately 1200 grams)
- Fresh lemon juice - 60 ml
- Feta cheese, crumbled - 85 grams
- Oregano - 1 tbsp
- Pepper
- Salt

DIRECTIONS:

1. Place chicken in a baking dish. Mix the remaining ingredients and pour over the chicken.
2. Place the baking dish into the air fryer basket.
3. Select Bake mode and cook at 180°C for 45 minutes.
4. Serve and enjoy.

PER SERVING: Calories 531, Carbs 1.49g, Fat 29.12g, Protein 62.12g

MEAT RECIPES

Meatballs

SERVES: 4 **COOK TIME: 8 minutes**

INGREDIENTS:
- Egg - 1
- Ground beef - 450 grams
- Italian seasoning - 1 tsp
- Onion powder - 2 tsp
- Fresh parsley, minced - 60 grams
- Breadcrumbs - 80 grams
- Parmesan cheese, grated - 60 grams
- Garlic cloves, minced - 2
- Ground pork - 110 grams
- Pepper
- Salt

DIRECTIONS:
1. Add all ingredients into the mixing bowl and mix until well combined.
2. Make equal shapes of balls from the meat mixture.
3. Arrange meatballs into an air fryer basket in a single layer.
4. Select Air Fry mode and cook at 200°C for 8 minutes.
5. Serve and enjoy.

PER SERVING: Calories 426, Carbs 5.16g, Fat 24.44g, Protein 43.85g

Juicy & Tender Pork Chops

SERVES: 4 **COOK TIME: 12 minutes**

INGREDIENTS:
- Pork chops, boneless - 4 (approximately 600 grams)
- Garlic powder - 1/4 tsp
- Onion powder - 1/2 tsp
- Italian seasoning - 1 tsp
- Olive oil - 10 ml
- Pepper
- Salt

DIRECTIONS:
1. Brush pork chops with oil and season with garlic powder, onion powder, Italian seasoning, pepper, and salt.
2. Place pork chops into the air fryer basket.
3. Select Air Fry mode and cook at 190°C for 12 minutes.
4. Serve and enjoy.

PER SERVING: Calories 357, Carbs 1.87g, Fat 19.64g, Protein 40.53g

Garlic Butter Pork Chops

INGREDIENTS: **SERVES: 4** **COOK TIME: 13 minutes**

- Pork chops, bone-in - 450 grams
- Garlic butter - 30 grams
- Brown sugar - 10 grams
- Olive oil - 5 ml
- Pepper - 1/4 tsp
- Salt - 1/2 tsp

DIRECTIONS:

1. Brush pork chops with oil and sprinkle with brown sugar, pepper, and salt.
2. Arrange pork chops into the air fryer basket.
3. Select Air Fry mode and cook at 200°C for 13 minutes. Flip pork chops halfway through.
4. Transfer pork chops onto a plate and top with garlic butter.
5. Serve and enjoy.

PER SERVING: Calories 304, Carbs 1.52g, Fat 19.43g, Protein 29.16g

Tasty Lamb Patties

INGREDIENTS: **SERVES: 4** **COOK TIME: 15 minutes**

- Ground lamb - 450 grams
- Ground allspice - 1/2 tsp
- Ground cinnamon - 1 tsp
- Fresh parsley, chopped - 60 ml
- Onion, minced - 60 grams
- Ground cumin - 1 tsp
- Garlic, minced - 15 grams
- Cayenne pepper - 1/4 tsp
- Ground coriander - 1 tsp
- Pepper
- Salt

DIRECTIONS:

1. Add meat and remaining ingredients into the mixing bowl and mix until well combined.
2. Place the crisper plate in the air fryer basket.
3. Make patties from the meat mixture and place them into the air fryer basket.
4. Select Bake mode and cook at 200°C for 15 minutes.
5. Serve and enjoy.

PER SERVING: Calories 232, Carbs 2.89g, Fat 14.29g, Protein 23.59g

Meatballs

SERVES: 4 **COOK TIME:** 20 minutes

INGREDIENTS:
- Egg, lightly beaten - 1
- Ground lamb - 450g
- Olive oil - 45ml
- Red pepper flakes - a pinch
- Ground cumin - 1 tsp
- Fresh oregano, chopped - 2 tsp
- Fresh parsley, chopped - 2 tbsp
- Garlic, minced - 1 tbsp
- Pepper - a pinch
- Kosher salt - 1 tsp

DIRECTIONS:
1. Add meat and remaining ingredients into the mixing bowl and mix until well combined.
2. Place the crisper plate in the air fryer basket.
3. Make balls from the meat mixture and place them into the air fryer basket.
4. Select Bake mode and cook at 200°C for 20 minutes.
5. Serve and enjoy.

PER SERVING: Calories 345, Carbs 2.12g, Fat 26.46g, Protein 25.32g

Garlic Mint Lamb Chops

INGREDIENTS: **SERVES:** 4 **COOK TIME:** 15 minutes

- Lamb loin chops - 12 (approximately 900 grams)
- Garlic cloves, minced - 6
- Fresh mint, chopped - 60 grams
- Olive oil - 120 ml
- Lime juice - 90 ml
- Lime zest - From 3 limes
- Pepper
- Salt

DIRECTIONS:
1. Add lamb chops and remaining ingredients into the large mixing bowl and mix well. Cover and place in refrigerator for 6 hours.
2. Remove lamb chops from the marinade and place into the air fryer basket.
3. Select Air Fry mode and cook at 190°C for 15 minutes.
4. Serve and enjoy.

PER SERVING: Calories 280, Carbs 5.65g, Fat 28.16g, Protein 3.18g

Mustard Lamb Chops

INGREDIENTS: **SERVES: 4**   **COOK TIME: 15 minutes**

- Loin lamb chops - 8 (approximately 600 grams)
- Fresh lemon juice - 15 ml
- Olive oil - 7.5 ml
- Mustard - 30 ml
- Tarragon - 1 tsp
- Pepper
- Salt

DIRECTIONS:

1. Add lamb chops and remaining ingredients into the mixing bowl and mix well. Cover and place in refrigerator for 2 hours.
2. Place marinated lamb chops into the air fryer basket.
3. Select Air Fry mode and cook at 200°C for 15 minutes.
4. Serve and enjoy.

PER SERVING: Calories 201, Carbs 1.86g, Fat 8.6g, Protein 27.71g

Balsamic Lamb Chops

INGREDIENTS: **SERVES: 4**   **COOK TIME: 15 minutes**

- Lamb chops - 450 grams
- Balsamic vinegar - 60 ml
- Garlic, crushed - 1 tsp
- Olive oil - 15 ml
- Onion powder - 1/2 tsp
- Paprika - 1/2 tsp
- Pepper
- Salt

DIRECTIONS:

1. Add lamb chops and remaining ingredients into the zip-lock bag. Seal the bag and place it in the refrigerator for 2 hours.
2. Place lamb chops into the air fryer basket.
3. Select Air Fry mode and cook at 200°C for 15 minutes.
4. Serve and enjoy.

PER SERVING: Calories 141, Carbs 4.41g, Fat 9.71g, Protein 8.81g

Garlic Sage Pork Chops

INGREDIENTS: **SERVES: 4**   **COOK TIME: 12 minutes**

- Pork chops - 4 (approximately 600 grams)
- Garlic, minced - 2 tsp
- Apple cider vinegar - 15 ml
- Dried sage - 1 tbsp
- Olive oil - 30 ml
- Pepper
- Salt

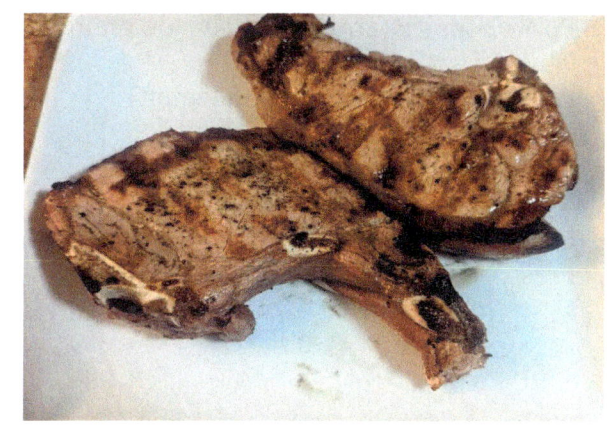

DIRECTIONS:

1. In a mixing bowl, mix pork chops with garlic, pepper, oil, sage, vinegar, and salt and set aside for 15 minutes.
2. Place pork chops into the air fryer basket.
3. Select Air Fry mode and cook at 200°C for 12 minutes.
4. Serve and enjoy.

PER SERVING: Calories 397, Carbs 1.87g, Fat 24.21g, Protein 40.57g

Steak Bites with Veggie

INGREDIENTS: **SERVES: 2**   **COOK TIME: 8 minutes**

- Ribeye steak, cut into cubes - 450 grams
- Mushrooms, sliced - 225 grams
- Garlic, minced - 15 grams
- Broccoli florets - 480 grams
- Butter, melted - 30 grams
- Worcestershire sauce - 1 tsp
- Pepper
- Salt

DIRECTIONS:

1. In a bowl, toss steak cubes with butter, broccoli, mushrooms, Worcestershire sauce, garlic, pepper, and salt.
2. Add the steak and vegetable mixture into the air fryer basket.
3. Select Air Fry mode and cook at 200°C for 8 minutes.
4. Serve and enjoy.

PER SERVING: Calories 577, Carbs 12.9g, Fat 38.02g, Protein 49.75g

Lemon Garlic Pork Chops

INGREDIENTS: **SERVES: 2** **COOK TIME: 15 minutes**

- Pork chops - 2 (approximately 300 grams)
- Olive oil - 15 ml
- Lemon zest, grated - From 1 lemon
- Garlic cloves, minced - 3
- Fresh rosemary, chopped - 2 tsp
- Red pepper flakes, crushed - 1/2 tsp
- Fennel seeds, crushed - 1 tsp
- Fresh sage, chopped - 1 tsp

DIRECTIONS:

1. In a small bowl, mix oil, red pepper flakes, lemon zest, garlic, fennel seeds, sage, rosemary, pepper, and salt.
2. Brush pork chops with oil mixture and place into the air fryer basket.
3. Select Air Fry mode and cook at 190°C for 15 minutes.
4. Serve and enjoy.

PER SERVING: Calories 415, Carbs 6.2g, Fat 24.48g, Protein 41.25g

Honey Mustard Pork Chops

INGREDIENTS: **SERVES: 4** **COOK TIME: 12 minutes**

- Pork chops, boneless - 450 grams
- Steak seasoning blend - 1 tsp
- Honey - 10 ml
- Yellow mustard - 15 ml

DIRECTIONS:

1. In a small bowl, mix mustard, honey, and steak seasoning.
2. Brush pork chops with mustard honey mixture and place into the air fryer basket.
3. Select Air Fry mode and cook at 180°C for 12 minutes. Turn pork chops halfway through.
4. Serve and enjoy.

PER SERVING: Calories 252, Carbs 3.55g, Fat 12.67g, Protein 29.23g

Sweet & Spicy Pork Chops

INGREDIENTS: **SERVES: 4**   **COOK TIME: 14 minutes**

- Pork chops - 4 (approximately 600 grams)
- Fresh lime juice - 30 ml
- Garlic, minced - 15 grams
- Olive oil - 15 ml
- Sweet chili sauce - 30 ml
- Honey - 60 ml
- Pepper
- Salt

DIRECTIONS:

1. Season pork chops with pepper and salt and place in an air fryer basket.
2. Select Air Fry mode and cook at 200°C for 10 minutes.
3. Meanwhile, heat oil in a pan over medium heat.
4. Add garlic and sauté for 30 seconds. Add lime juice, chilli sauce, and honey and cook until sauce thickens, about 3-4 minutes.
5. Place pork chops on a plate.
6. Pour sauce over pork chops.
7. Serve and enjoy.

PER SERVING: Calories 436, Carbs 20.72g, Fat 20.79g, Protein 40.77g

Mexican Meat Patties

INGREDIENTS: **SERVES: 4**   **COOK TIME: 10 minutes**

- Egg - 1
- Ground beef - 450 grams
- Onions, chopped - 60 grams
- Cheddar cheese, shredded - 60 grams
- Taco seasoning - 2 tbsp
- Pepper
- Salt

DIRECTIONS:

1. Add meat and remaining ingredients into the mixing bowl and mix until well combined.
2. Make equal shapes of patties from the meat mixture and place them into the air fryer basket.
3. Select Air Fry mode and cook at 200°C for 10 minutes.
4. Serve and enjoy.

PER SERVING: Calories 296, Carbs 4.47g, Fat 15.03g, Protein 32.93g

Beef Jerky

INGREDIENTS: **SERVES:** 6   **COOK TIME:** 8 hours

- Flank steak, cut into thin slices - 900 grams
- Ranch seasoning (a mix of parsley, dill weed, garlic powder, onion powder, basil, and black pepper) - 45 grams
- Worcestershire sauce - 180 ml
- Soy sauce - 180 ml
- Cayenne - 1/4 tsp
- Liquid smoke - 5 ml
- Red pepper flakes - 3 tsp

DIRECTIONS:

1. Add steak slices and remaining ingredients into the large bowl and mix well, cover, and place in the refrigerator overnight.
2. Arrange steak slices into the air fryer basket in a single layer. Place the crisper plate in the air fryer basket and arrange the remaining steak slices on the crisper plate.
3. Select Dehydrate mode and cook at 60°C for 8 hours.
4. Serve and enjoy.

PER SERVING: Calories 341, Carbs 17.29g, Fat 13.35g, Protein 34.9g

Meatballs

INGREDIENTS: **SERVES:** 8   **COOK TIME:** 10 minutes

- Egg - 2, lightly beaten
- Ground beef - 900 grams
- Fresh parsley, chopped - 120 grams
- Garlic, minced - 15 grams
- Onion, chopped - 1
- Worcestershire sauce - 1 tbsp
- Feta cheese crumbled - 120 grams
- Breadcrumbs - 120 grams

DIRECTIONS:

1. Add all ingredients into the mixing bowl and mix until well combined.
2. Make small balls from the meat mixture and place them into the air fryer basket.
3. Select Air Fry mode and cook at 200°C for 10 minutes.
4. Serve and enjoy.

PER SERVING: Calories 308, Carbs 3.52g, Fat 16.72g, Protein 33.79g

Herb Pork Chops

INGREDIENTS: **SERVES: 2** **COOK TIME: 14 minutes**

- Pork chops - 2 (approximately 300 grams)
- Oregano - 1 tsp
- Thyme - 1 tsp
- Sage - 1 tsp
- Olive oil - 15 ml
- Garlic powder - 1/2 tsp
- Paprika - 1/2 tsp
- Rosemary - 1/2 tsp
- Pepper
- Salt

DIRECTIONS:

1. Brush pork chops with oil.
2. In a small bowl, mix oregano, thyme, sage, garlic powder, paprika, rosemary, pepper, and salt and rub over pork chops.
3. Place pork chops into the air fryer basket.
4. Select Air Fry mode and cook at 180°C for 14 minutes. Turn pork chops halfway through.
5. Serve and enjoy.

PER SERVING: Calories 404, Carbs 3.73g, Fat 24.33g, Protein 40.99g

Marinated Pork ribs

INGREDIENTS: **SERVES: 4** **COOK TIME: 40 minutes**

- Baby pork ribs - 450 grams
- Olive oil - 15 ml
- Ginger paste - 1 tsp
- Garlic paste - 1 tsp
- Worcestershire sauce – 1 tbsp
- Hoisin sauce - 2 tsp

DIRECTIONS:

1. Add meat and remaining ingredients into the mixing bowl and coat well. Cover and place in the refrigerator for 2 hours.
2. Place marinated ribs into the air fryer basket.
3. Select Air Fry mode and cook at 150°C for 40 minutes. Turn ribs halfway through.
4. Serve and enjoy.

PER SERVING: Calories 201, Carbs 2.67g, Fat 9.92g, Protein 23.76g

Meatballs

INGREDIENTS: **SERVES: 6**   **COOK TIME: 12 minutes**

- Egg - 1
- Ground beef – 550 grams
- Garlic cloves, minced - 6
- Olive oil – 30 ml
- Flour – 90 grams
- Basil, chopped – 30 grams
- Parsley, chopped – 30 grams
- Parmesan cheese, grated – 60 grams
- Almond milk – 120 ml
- Pepper - 1 tsp
- Salt - 1 tsp

DIRECTIONS:

1. Add meat and remaining ingredients into the mixing bowl and mix until well combined.
2. Place the crisper plate in the air fryer basket
3. Make balls from the meat mixture and place them into the air fryer basket.
4. Select Bake mode and cook at 180 C for 12 minutes.
5. Serve and enjoy.

PER SERVING: Calories 431, Carbs 4.12g, Fat 37.55g, Protein 18.49g

Pork Jerky

INGREDIENTS: **SERVES: 4**   **COOK TIME: 5 hours**

- Pork lean meat, sliced thinly - 450 grams
- Paprika - 1 tsp
- Garlic powder - 1/2 tsp
- Pepper - 1/4 tsp
- Oregano - 1/2 tsp
- Chili powder - 1 tsp
- Salt - 1 tsp

DIRECTIONS:

1. Add meat slices and remaining ingredients into the large mixing bowl and mix well. Cover and place in the refrigerator overnight.
2. Arrange meat slices into the air fryer basket in a single layer. Place the crisper plate in the air fryer basket and arrange the remaining meat slices on the crisper plate.
3. Select Dehydrate mode and cook at 70°C for 5 hours.
4. Serve and enjoy.

PER SERVING: Calories 597, Carbs 10.06g, Fat 17.88g, Protein 103.56g

VEGETABLE RECIPES

Courgette Casserole

INGREDIENTS: **SERVES: 6** **COOK TIME: 45 minutes**

- Egg whites - 2
- Breadcrumbs – 60 grams
- Parmesan cheese, grated – 25 grams
- Feta cheese, crumbled – 25 grams
- Courgette, diced - 4 small
- Spinach – 675 grams
- Dried basil - 1 tsp
- Pepper - 1/2 tsp
- Garlic powder - 2 tsp
- Olive oil - 2 tbsp
- Kosher salt - 1/2 tsp

DIRECTIONS:

1. Heat oil in a pan over medium heat.
2. Add spinach and courgette and cook for 5 minutes.
3. Transfer the spinach mixture to the mixing bowl.
4. Add all remaining ingredients to the mixing bowl and mix well.
5. Pour the mixture into the greased baking dish. Place the baking dish into the air fryer basket.
6. Select Bake mode and cook at 200°C for 40 minutes.
7. Serve and enjoy.

PER SERVING: Calories 90, Carbs 2.85g, Fat 7.12g, Protein 4.17g

Baked Brussels Sprouts

INGREDIENTS: **SERVES: 6** **COOK TIME: 30 minutes**

- Brussels sprouts, halved – 350 grams
- Cayenne - 1/4 tsp
- Chili powder - 1/4 tsp
- Garlic powder - 1/4 tsp
- Olive oil – 60 ml
- Salt - 1/4 tsp

DIRECTIONS:

1. Add all ingredients into the mixing bowl and toss well.
2. Place the crisper plate in the air fryer basket.
3. Transfer Brussels sprouts into the air fryer basket.
4. Select Bake mode and cook at 200°C for 30 minutes. Stir Brussels sprouts halfway through.
5. Serve and enjoy.

PER SERVING: Calories 93, Carbs 2.83g, Fat 9.12g, Protein 1.04g

Healthy Baked Vegetables

INGREDIENTS: **SERVES: 4** **COOK TIME: 35 minutes**

- Brussels sprouts, cut in half – 350 grams
- Mushrooms, cut in half – 225 grams
- Onion, cut into wedges - 1
- Courgette, cut into 1/2-inch slices - 2
- Bell peppers, cut into 2-inch chunks - 2
- Balsamic Vinegar - 2 tbsp
- Olive oil – 60 ml
- Salt - 1/2 tsp

DIRECTIONS:

1. Add vegetables to the large mixing bowl. Mix vinegar, oil, and salt and pour over vegetables.
2. Cover the bowl and place it in the refrigerator for 1 hour.
3. Place the crisper plate in the air fryer basket.
4. Add vegetables into the air fryer basket.
5. Select Bake mode and cook at 190°C for 35 minutes. Stir halfway through.
6. Serve and enjoy.

PER SERVING: Calories 198, Carbs 16.35g, Fat 14.02g, Protein 5.15g

Cheesy Courgette Bake

INGREDIENTS: **SERVES: 6** **COOK TIME: 30 minutes**

- Courgettes, sliced - 4 medium
- Tomatoes, sliced - 3
- Olive oil - 1 tbsp
- Parmesan cheese, shredded – 150 grams
- Pepper
- Salt

DIRECTIONS:

1. Arrange courgette slices and tomato slices in the baking dish.
2. Drizzle with olive oil and season with pepper and salt. Sprinkle Parmesan cheese on top of vegetables.
3. Place the baking dish in the air fryer basket.
4. Select Bake mode and cook at 180°C for 30 minutes.
5. Serve and enjoy.

PER SERVING: Calories 96, Carbs 3.55g, Fat 6.95g, Protein 5.15g

Carrot Courgette Patties

INGREDIENTS: **SERVES: 2** **COOK TIME: 15 minutes**

- Egg - 1
- Courgette, grated & squeezed - 1
- Carrot, grated & squeezed - 1
- Parmesan cheese, grated – 80 grams
- Breadcrumbs – 80 grams
- Pepper
- Salt

DIRECTIONS:

1. Add all ingredients into the bowl and mix until well combined.
2. Make patties from the mixture and place them in an air fryer basket.
3. Select Air Fry mode and cook at 200°C for 15 minutes.
4. Serve and enjoy.

PER SERVING: Calories 135, Carbs 6.44g, Fat 8.41g, Protein 8.81g

Crispy Cauliflower Florets

INGREDIENTS: **SERVES: 4** **COOK TIME: 20 minutes**

- Cauliflower florets – 625 grams
- Cumin powder - 1/2 tsp
- Ground coriander - 1/2 tsp
- Garlic cloves, chopped - 5
- Olive oil – 60 ml
- Salt - 1/2 tsp

DIRECTIONS:

1. Add cauliflower florets and remaining ingredients into the mixing bowl and toss well.
2. Add cauliflower florets into the air fryer basket.
3. Select Air Fry mode and cook at 200°C for 20 minutes. Stir cauliflower florets halfway through.
4. Serve and enjoy.

PER SERVING: Calories 159, Carbs 8.01g, Fat 13.95g, Protein 2.86g

Garlic Mushrooms

INGREDIENTS: **SERVES: 4** **COOK TIME: 15 minutes**

- Baby portobello mushrooms, halved – 425 grams
- Garlic, minced - 2 tsp
- Butter, melted – 30 grams
- Coconut aminos (if you are unable to get hold of this, use soy sauce instead) - 2 tsp
- Pepper
- Salt

DIRECTIONS:

1. In a mixing bowl, toss mushrooms with garlic, coconut aminos, butter, pepper, and salt.
2. Add the mushroom mixture to the air fryer basket.
3. Select Air Fry mode and cook at 200°C for 15 minutes.
4. Serve and enjoy.

PER SERVING: Calories 89, Carbs 6.34g, Fat 6.41g, Protein 3.88g

Spinach Quinoa Patties

INGREDIENTS: **SERVES: 10** **COOK TIME: 10 minutes**

- Egg - 1
- Spinach, chopped – 225 grams
- Quinoa, cooked – 375 grams
- Breadcrumbs – 115 grams
- Onion, chopped – 120 grams
- Carrot, peel & shredded – 120 grams
- Garlic, minced - 1 tsp
- Parmesan cheese, grated – 25 grams
- Milk – 60 ml
- Parsley, minced - 2 tbsp
- Pepper
- Salt

DIRECTIONS:

1. Add quinoa and remaining ingredients into the mixing bowl and mix until well combined.
2. Make patties from the quinoa mixture and place them into the air fryer basket.
3. Select Air Fry mode and cook at 190°C for 10 minutes.
4. Serve and enjoy.

PER SERVING: Calories 120, Carbs 4.97g, Fat 10.7g, Protein 1.71g

Crispy Sweet Potato Wedges

INGREDIENTS: **SERVES: 4** **COOK TIME: 16 minutes**

- Sweet potatoes, scrubbed & cut into wedges - 2 small
- Parmesan cheese, grated – 35 grams
- Chili powder - 1/8 tsp
- Paprika - 1/4 tsp
- Garlic powder - 1/4 tsp
- Olive oil – 30 ml
- Pepper - 1/4 tsp
- Salt - 1/2 tsp

DIRECTIONS:

1. In a mixing bowl, toss sweet potatoes with the remaining ingredients until well coated.
2. Add sweet potato mixture to the air fryer basket.
3. Select Air Fry mode and cook at 200°C for 16 minutes. Shake the basket halfway through.
4. Serve and enjoy.

PER SERVING: Calories 124, Carbs 7.9g, Fat 9.13g, Protein 3.07g

Tomato Slices

INGREDIENTS: **SERVES: 4** **COOK TIME: 12 hours**

- Tomatoes, thinly sliced - 4 medium
- Pepper
- Salt

DIRECTIONS:

1. Arrange tomato slices into the air fryer basket in a single layer. Place the crisper plate in the air fryer basket and arrange the remaining tomato slices on the crisper plate.
2. Select Dehydrate mode and cook at 60°C for 12 hours.
3. Serve and enjoy.

PER SERVING: Calories 7, Carbs 1.65g, Fat 0.05g, Protein 0.36g

DESSERTS

Tender & Sweet Cinnamon Apples

INGREDIENTS: **SERVES: 4**   **COOK TIME: 15 minutes**

- Apples, peeled, cored & cut into cubes - 2 large
- Ground cinnamon - 1/4 tsp
- Brown sugar – 1 tbsp
- Butter, melted – 15 grams
- Pinch of salt

DIRECTIONS:

1. In a mixing bowl, toss apples with melted butter until well coated.
2. Arrange apple cubes into the air fryer basket.
3. Select Air Fry mode and cook at 200°C for 15 minutes.
4. Transfer cooked apple cubes into the mixing bowl. Sprinkle cinnamon, brown sugar, and salt on the top and toss well to coat.
5. Serve and enjoy.

PER SERVING: Calories 92, Carbs 17.54g, Fat 3.07g, Protein 0.33g

Delicious Berry Brownie

INGREDIENTS: **SERVES: 12**   **COOK TIME: 25 minutes**

- Eggs - 3
- Coconut cream, melted – 240 ml
- Honey – 120 ml
- Fresh raspberries – 120 grams
- Coffee – 1 tbsp
- Cinnamon – 1 tbsp
- Cocoa powder – 2 tbsp
- Baking soda - 1/2 tsp
- Vanilla - 2 tsp
- Pinch of salt

DIRECTIONS:

1. In a bowl, whisk together eggs, coffee, cinnamon, cocoa powder, baking soda, salt, vanilla, and honey.
2. Add raspberries to the egg mixture and fold well.
3. Pour the mixture into the greased baking pan. Place the baking pan into the air fryer basket.
4. Select Bake mode and cook at 165°C for 25 minutes. Drizzle coconut cream over the brownie.
5. Slice and serve.

PER SERVING: Calories 168, Carbs 29.59g, Fat 9.66g, Protein 3.5g

Date Brownies

SERVES: 16 **COOK TIME: 20 minutes**

INGREDIENTS:
- Dates, pitted – 160 grams
- Almond flour – 90 grams
- Vanilla - 2 tsp
- Honey – 45 ml
- Baking powder - 1/2 tsp
- Cocoa powder – 60 grams
- Hot water – 180 ml
- Pinch of sea salt

DIRECTIONS:
1. Add dates and hot water to a bowl and allow to sit for 10 minutes. Drain well.
2. Add soaked dates into the food processor and process until smooth.
3. Add almond flour, vanilla, honey, cocoa powder, and salt into the food processor and process until smooth.
4. Pour mixture into the 8 x 8-inch greased baking dish. Place the baking dish into the air fryer basket.
5. Select Bake mode and cook at 180°C for 20 minutes.
6. Slice and serve.

PER SERVING: Calories 46, Carbs 11.78g, Fat 0.42g, Protein 0.74g

Vanilla Berry Cobbler

SERVES: 6 **COOK TIME: 15 minutes**

INGREDIENTS:
- Egg, lightly beaten - 1
- Blackberries, sliced – 120 grams
- Butter, melted – 15 grams
- Almond flour – 120 grams
- Truvia (sweetener) - 2 tsp
- Vanilla - 1/2 tsp

DIRECTIONS:
1. Add blackberries to the baking dish. Sprinkle sweetener over blackberries.
2. Mix almond flour, butter, and vanilla in the bowl.
3. Add egg to almond flour mixture and stir well to combine.
4. Spread almond flour mixture over blackberries. Place the baking dish into the air fryer basket.
5. Select Bake mode and cook at 180°C for 15 minutes.
6. Serve and enjoy.

PER SERVING: Calories 77, Carbs 10.35g, Fat 3.46g, Protein 1.67g

Orange Muffins

SERVES: 12 **COOK TIME: 15 minutes**

INGREDIENTS:

- Eggs - 4
- Orange, juiced - 1
- Butter, melted – 120 grams
- Almond flour – 360 grams
- Baking soda - 1 tsp
- Orange zest - from 1 orange

DIRECTIONS:

1. Line the muffin pans with cupcake liners and set aside.
2. Add all ingredients into the large bowl and mix until well combined.
3. Pour the mixture into the prepared muffin pan. Place the muffin pan into the air fryer basket.
4. Select Bake mode and cook at 180°C for 20 minutes.
5. Serve and enjoy.

PER SERVING: Calories 123, Carbs 2.8g, Fat 11.06g, Protein 3.27g

Almond Butter Banana Brownie

SERVES: 4 **COOK TIME: 16 minutes**

INGREDIENTS:

- Protein powder - 1 scoop
- Almond butter, melted – 120 ml
- Cocoa powder – 2 tbsp
- Bananas, overripe – 240 ml

DIRECTIONS:

1. Add all ingredients into the blender and blend until smooth.
2. Pour batter into the greased cake pan. Place the cake pan into the air fryer basket.
3. Select Bake mode and cook at 160°C for 16 minutes.
4. Serve and enjoy.

PER SERVING: Calories 321, Carbs 25.04g, Fat 24.57g, Protein 4.83g

Dehydrated Mango Slices

INGREDIENTS: **SERVES: 4** **COOK TIME: 12 hours**

- Mangoes, peeled and cut into 1/4-inch-thick slices - 2

DIRECTIONS:

1. Arrange mango slices into the air fryer basket in a single layer. Place the crisper plate in the air fryer basket and arrange the remaining mango slices on the crisper plate.
2. Select Dehydrate mode and cook at 60°C for 12 hours.
3. Serve and enjoy.

PER SERVING: Calories 101, Carbs 25.17g, Fat 0.64g, Protein 1.38g

Banana Muffins

INGREDIENTS: **SERVES: 8** **COOK TIME: 10 minutes**

- Egg - 1
- Sugar – 45 grams
- Butter – 55 grams
- Banana, mashed - 1
- Walnuts, chopped – 30 grams
- Baking powder - 1/4 tsp
- All-purpose flour – 95 grams
- Vanilla - 1/4 tsp

DIRECTIONS:

1. In a bowl, beat butter and sugar until smooth. Add mashed banana, egg, and vanilla and beat well.
2. Add flour and baking powder and mix until well combined. Add walnuts and fold well.
3. Spoon batter into the greased muffin pan. Place the pan into the air fryer basket.
4. Select Bake mode and cook at 180°C for 10 minutes.
5. Serve and enjoy.

PER SERVING: Calories 138, Carbs 12.43g, Fat 8.68g, Protein 2g

Dehydrated Apple Slices

INGREDIENTS: **SERVES: 4**   **COOK TIME: 8 hours**

- Apples, cored and cut into 1/8-inch-thick slices - 2
- Cinnamon - 1 tsp

DIRECTIONS:

1. Arrange apple slices into the air fryer basket in a single layer. Place the crisper plate in the air fryer basket and arrange the remaining apple slices on the crisper plate.
2. Sprinkle cinnamon on top of apple slices.
3. Select Dehydrate mode and cook at 60°C for 8 hours.
4. Serve and enjoy.

PER SERVING: Calories 70, Carbs 17.7g, Fat 0.45g, Protein 0.21g

Kiwi Slices

INGREDIENTS: **SERVES: 4**   **COOK TIME: 12 hours**

- Kiwis, peeled & cut into 1/4-inch-thick slices - 2

DIRECTIONS:

1. Arrange kiwi slices into the air fryer basket in a single layer. Place the crisper plate in the air fryer basket and arrange the remaining kiwi slices on the crisper plate.
2. Select Dehydrate mode and cook at 60°C for 12 hours.
3. Serve and enjoy.

PER SERVING: Calories 0, Carbs 0.08g, Fat 0.01g, Protein 0.02g

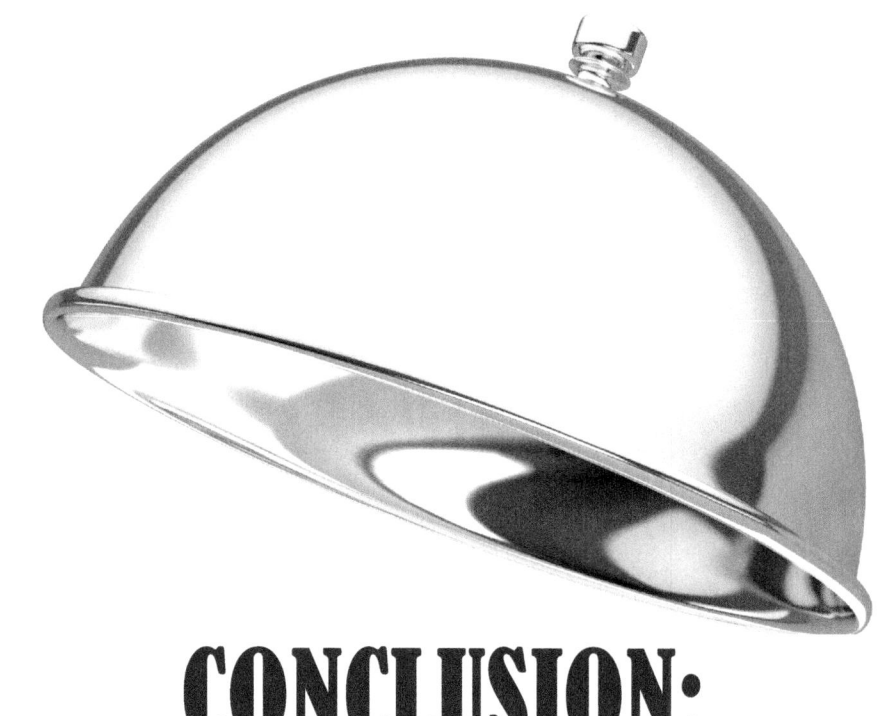

CONCLUSION:

In conclusion, the Ninja Air Fryer Cookbook is like a key that opens the door to an adventure full of tasty and healthy recipes. Whether you are a cooking professional or just beginning, this cookbook for the Ninja Air Fryer, makes cooking easy and fun. Try out different things with your air fryer, like max crisp, air fry, air roast, air broil, bake, reheat, and dehydrating. Enjoy a bunch of recipes, from breakfast to desserts. This cookbook is all about cooking in an efficient way and offers clear instructions to make cooking simple. Say bye to tasteless food and welcome a world of yummy textures and flavours. Cheers to the pleasure of air frying and making delicious meals with ease!

This page is for your notes

This page is for your notes

Printed in Great Britain
by Amazon